HANDY POCKET GUIDE

CREWEL EMBROIDERY

Jo Avery

Everything to Get You Started

5 Samplers

C&T P[...]
Anothe[...]

CONTENTS

INTRODUCTION

CREWEL EMBROIDERY

The word crewel is an old English or Welsh word meaning wool, which was the traditional material for embroidery. Beginning in the Jacobean era (1603–1625), crewelwork was popular throughout the seventeenth century with traditional crewelwork often referred to by that name. Twisted two-ply wool thread was used to decorate clothing and home furnishings with many of the same stitches still being used today to recreate the look. Traditional crewelwork stitches take advantage of the thickness of wool to create a raised, dimensional feel to the work. In the following collection of sampler embroideries, I have tried to exploit this added texture while offering a new modern twist, simplifying the stitches and aesthetic. Wool is a great choice for embroidery because it works up quickly and the fluffy threads hide imperfections more readily than cotton or silk.

You need little in the way of equipment or material to embark on your first embroidery. As well as accessibility, this means much less impact on the environment than other crafts, such as quilting, especially when wool and linen are chosen over cotton. I have made a conscious effort to use as much natural product as possible in this book. Even though I hope my embroideries will become treasured heirlooms, I am also comforted to know that they will biodegrade easily at some future stage without harming our planet.

Embroidery is not the most forgiving of crafts as your stitching is on display, not hidden as in other sewing. When I first began embroidering, I was in too much of a hurry to finish, my stitching was a little slapdash, and therefore I was not satisfied with the results. I had to learn to slow down and become neater with my stitches. I had to be prepared to take some stitches out if they were not even and try again. Embroidery rewards patience and dedication, and the key is to embrace the slowness rather than begrudge it and enjoy the process as much as the end result. This slow meditative stitching has huge benefits for your mental health, providing the perfect activity to practice mindfulness. You will find yourself calmed and relaxed by the repetitive action of coloring-in with stitches and threads.

HOW TO USE THIS BOOK

The wide range of projects in this book makes it suitable for new embroiderers while hopefully appealing to those who have been stitching for years. All the patterns in this book are samplers, traditionally designed to show off a range of stitches and the skills of the embroiderer. Each sampler is made up of similar shapes, which are each filled with different stitches. The five designs can then be turned into a range of imaginative small projects or framed as pictures if you prefer. The stitches are explained at the start as an easy reference.

I have also used felt appliqué to fill some of the shapes on two of the projects. If you like this approach, you can add felt to more of the designs. Once you get the hang of the stitches, I would encourage you to create your own versions, filling areas with whichever stitch you like and not following my instructions too rigorously.

Each of the stitches is referred to by the same identifying number throughout, and you will soon learn that a "2" means satin stitch and so on, which will help you decipher the stitch guides. The colors are listed by letter and these change with each pattern. Some stitches, such as laid work, usually include two contrasting colors, and these are indicated on the guides by a slash as in "D/F." The first letter will always be the prominent color with the second being the smaller detail. If the specific colors called out are no longer available, substitute with your desired color. Of course, you are most welcome to use whichever thread or color you like, wherever you like!

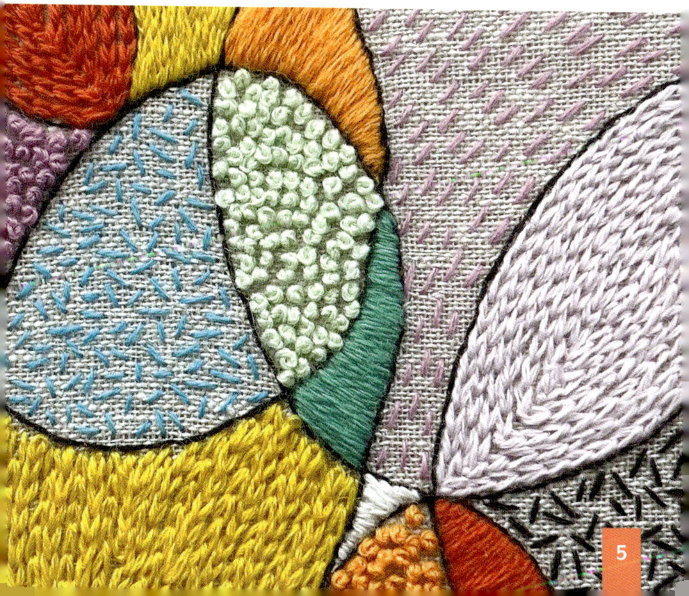

Play around with your favorite stitches and colors to create your own version of the projects. Here's a variation of Doodle Hoop (page 35)

MATERIALS AND EQUIPMENT

FABRICS

You can embroider onto any sort of fabric you like, though textiles with a looser weave tend to be easier to work with. As I come from a quilting background, I like to use the same linen/cotton mix fabrics that I can also use for patchwork instead of buying specially made embroidery linens. Specialist embroidery linens tend to be stiffer and more unyielding. I like to use Essex Linen by Robert Kaufman, which has a firm stable feel while retaining softness and pliability and is available in a wide variety of shades and finishes. For the designs that will end up as pictures in hoops, you can chance lighter fabrics, such as the hand-dyed cotton I used for the Mandala Hoop (page 47) and Bubbles Hoop (page 39), as they will stay permanently stabilized. There is a wide variety of stabilizer materials available that can help with lighter fabric, but I prefer to stitch without and simply match the fabric with the project by suitability.

THREAD

I have used Aurifil 12-weight wool thread for most of the projects in the book. One of the things I love about the Aurifil wool thread is that it comes on spools rather than skeins and is much easier to handle. As a naturally untidy person, I have always found embroidery skeins very frustrating to use and store.

Most of the stitches are worked with two strands of Aurifil wool thread. I start by cutting one long piece that is double the length of a usual strand, and then I thread one end though the needle before knotting the two ends together. This works perfectly for me and the strands rarely separate or twist. The usual advice when cutting a single strand of thread is to knot the end you cut from the spool, which ensures a smoother thread. However, the way I double my thread means that it will run in both directions. Having also experimented with two strands parallel and threaded together through the needle, I can confirm that with wool thread it makes no difference that I can discern.

All the designs can be stitched with regular stranded cotton floss or perle cotton and will look equally beautiful, so if you prefer to use your current stock of embroidery threads, please go ahead with my blessing. To help you use other threads, I have compiled a conversion chart from Aurifil wool to DMC cotton, which is on my website (see About the Author, page 63).

NEEDLES

Crewel needles are designed for embroidery floss, being of medium length with a sharp point and a long eye to accommodate several thicknesses of thread. These are perfect for the thicker crewel wool and linen threads. But I prefer to use sharps needles in a size 4 or 5 eye for the finer Aurifil wool thread. They have a smaller round eye and can also be used for any general hand sewing in the book. Choose a good brand of needle, such as Milward, John James, or Tulip.

HOOPS

My preferred hoop is wooden and made by Elbesee. These have a slot in the end of their tightening screw, designed to take a slotted screwdriver, and this enables you to tighten your hoop in a way you couldn't achieve with just the power of your grip. I have suggested a size of hoop for each project, but the choice is a personal one. I find if I choose too large a hoop, it can be difficult to reach the center of the design, making it awkward for some stitches, such as knots. If I choose a smaller hoop, the design might not fit completely, meaning the inconvenience of moving the hoop halfway through stitching. For a special project, I often use a fancier hoop for permanent framing, such as the gorgeous range by Auburn Hoops.

MARKING PENS

Most of the designs need to be traced onto the linen, using lines that you may want to remove later in case anything is still seen after the embroidery is finished. My preferred tool is a Pilot FriXion pen where the marks become invisible with heat from an iron. However, the marks don't go away and can reappear if your embroidery becomes very cold, such as in the hold of an aircraft (something to consider if you are gifting your embroidery overseas!). It can also leave a "ghost line," though this is less of a problem with embroidery where the marks will be too close to the stitching for this to show.

There are many other erasable pens available, some that are removed with water, others by air, and I would encourage you to experiment with different methods. For marking on dark fabric, I recommend a Clover white marking pen, which is designed for Sashiko. Always test your marking pens on a scrap of fabric first.

NOTIONS

Here are a few other useful items that may become indispensable to you as you work through this book.

Small sharp pair of scissors

Needle threader

Seam ripper

Tracing wheel—for marking felt

Screwdriver—for tightening hoops

Appliqué pins—tiny pins, perfect for holding felt appliqué pieces in place while stitching

TECHNIQUES

ENLARGING OR DOWNLOADING

The patterns in this pocket guide need to be enlarged. The percentage for enlargement is with each pattern as well as a 1″ guide. Use that 1″ guide to check the accuracy of your enlargement.

The patterns are also available full-size as downloads. Use the QR code at right or go to this site for your downloads and instructions:

tinyurl.com/20558-patterns-download

TRACING

Once your pattern is enlarged or downloaded, tracing from the pattern using a lightbox is the quickest and easiest way to transfer the design onto fabric. These days, lightboxes are relatively cheap and readily available at craft stores. Use masking tape to secure both the design and the fabric on top, making sure the fabric is square, that is, that the grain is aligned horizontally and vertically and well stretched. You can make your own temporary lightbox by taking a small shallow cardboard box with no lid (such as a shoebox) and putting your phone inside with the torch function switched on. Place a piece of glass or acrylic, such as a large square patchwork ruler, on the box and trace your pattern on top of this.

The Mandala and the Clamshell Pillow designs are given as half of a mirror image to fit within the book page. For these you will need to first trace the design by turning the pattern over so that it is facedown on the lightbox, and draw over the outlines onto the paper. Then trace the pattern from the book again, faceup, onto a separate sheet before taping the two pieces together, aligning the sides to give a perfect mirror image.

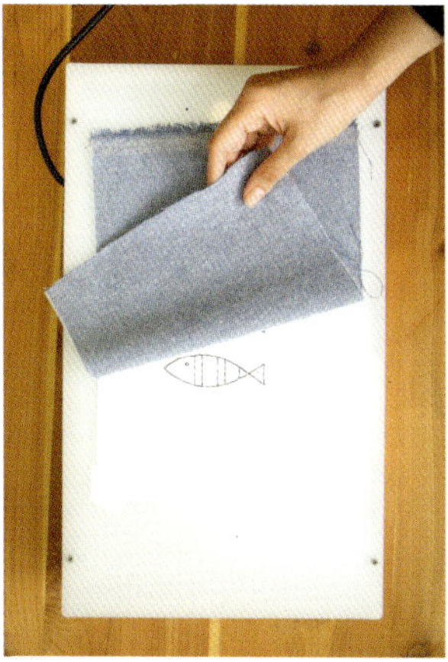

Preparing to trace from pattern to fabric, using a lightbox

Marking Felt

It is almost impossible to see through a dense layer of wool felt, even with a lightbox, so try using a dressmaker's tracing wheel instead. Lay your felt down on top of one or two spare layers of felt and place the paper pattern on top. Trace the lines by pressing down hard on the wheel through the paper. When you take the

Marking felt using a tracing wheel

paper away, there should be enough indentations for you to see the pattern clearly. You can now use your usual marking pen to fill in the lines.

HOOPING

Inserting the Fabric

Once you have the design on the fabric, insert it into a suitable embroidery hoop.

Take a while to position your fabric correctly, pulling and tightening by turn to make sure your fabric is as tight as possible; it should feel like a drum skin. Use a slotted screwdriver to obtain the correct tightness on the fixing screw. If your embroidery is not intended to stay in the hoop, and if you think you may take a while to finish it, you might like to use a fabric tape to bind the inner ring of your hoop. This prevents marking the fabric and helps hold the fabric securely.

Once it's stitched, you should remove the embroidery from the hoop and press it carefully from the back, using low heat. If you are using wool thread, you need to be extra careful not to scorch the wool. If you need to press from the front as well (to remove stubborn pen marks for instance), I advise placing a pressing cloth, such as a clean tea towel, on top of your embroidery for extra protection.

Finishing a Hoop Back

If your embroidery is going to be framed in the hoop, then re-insert as before. Press the excess fabric to the back and trim away all but ½" (1cm) from the edge.

Place a piece of scrap fabric, suitable for the lining, underneath and draw around using the outer edge of the hoop. Cut this fabric circle out and press over ¼" (6mm) seam all the way around the edge (toward the wrong side).

* TIP *

Before stitching the lining in place, I like to put a piece of scrap batting inside the hoop, which I simply cut roughly to size by eye. In some lights, you can see through the linen to the back of the work, and this optional step will help avoid the see-through.

Pin the lining, right side up, to the ½" (1cm) of the remaining linen. Stitch all the way around using a slip stitch, pulling the two fabrics together firmly with each stitch.

If your hoop isn't a snug fit, you may need to lace your hoop before finishing the back to pull the linen together. Use the strongest thread you can find and take a stitch first at one side of the linen and then the other. Pull the thread tight every few stitches. Repeat to lace the remaining opposite sides together.

* TIP *

To give your embroidery frame a special touch, try painting a wooden hoop in a color that matches your embroidery.

STARTING AND FINISHING

When working on The Great Tapestry of Scotland, we were warned never to leave knots in the work. Over time and in different temperatures and climates, the threads may move and tighten, and for something that was being stitched for posterity, this was especially important. Therefore, I learned to start stitching using the "waste knot" method and have used this ever since.

Start with a knot on the front of your work, which you will eventually cut off once the thread has been secured by stitches. Make a knot in the end of the thread and insert the needle from the right side, within the area that will be covered by stitching. Work the stitches to fill the area, securing the thread on the back at the same time. Then carefully cut the knot when you reach it. This can seem a tricky maneuver when you are beginning a piece, especially with your first line of backstitch outline; so keep checking the back and, if necessary, use your needle to weave around the excess thread there and make sure it is caught. Once areas of the design are stitched, you can also weave your starting thread through the stitching at the back, while keeping the knot on the front until it is safe to cut off.

To finish off a thread, simply weave the thread in and out of the stitches at the back of your work before cutting any excess. When using a very stable fabric, such as felt, there is no need to worry about leaving knots long term, so feel free to start with a simple knot at the back and immediately start stitching.

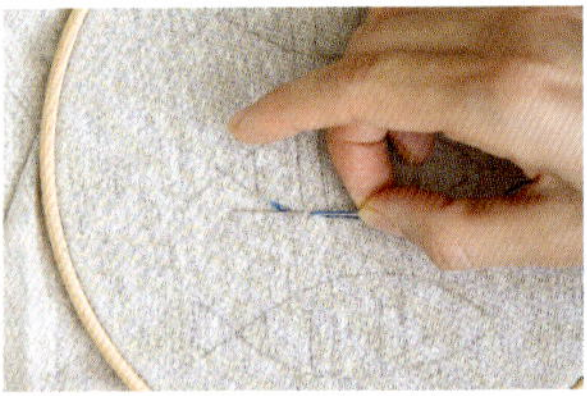

Starting knot

OUTLINE STITCHES

All the projects in this book are outlined with a backstitch. It is my favorite method and gives a clean graphic line.

Backstitch

Working from right to left, bring the needle up through the fabric at A, then back through at B, which will be the actual start of the outline. Bring the needle up again at C, a stitch length in front of A. Repeat the process, going back in again at A, then forward, a stitch length in front at D. Aim to keep each stitch length the same for an even appearance.

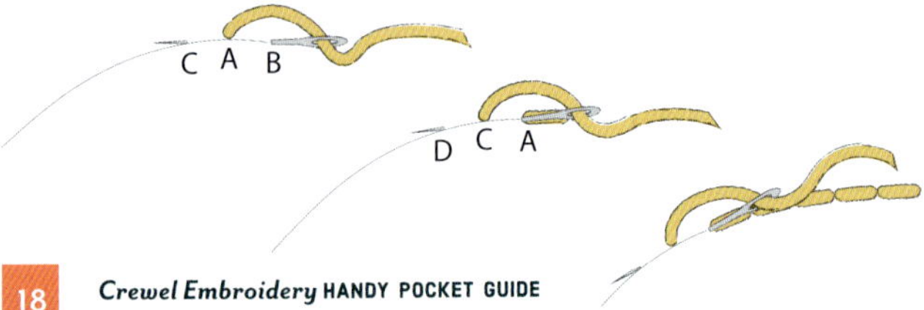

Whipped Backstitch

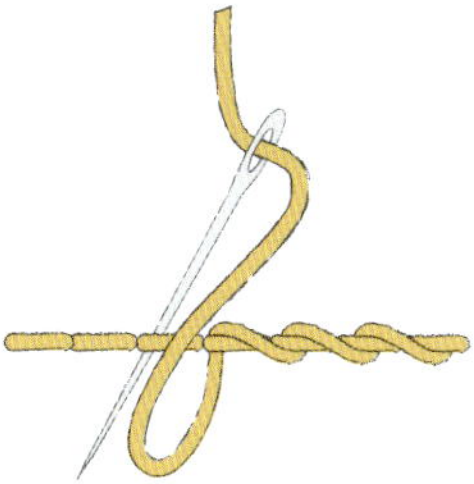

This extra step gives more emphasis to the outline. Whipping the backstitch will also hide any imperfections and smooth out unevenness of stitches, so feel free to use it even if not instructed in the pattern. It's a very helpful extra step for beginner embroiderers and hides a multitude of sins! Bring the needle up at one end of the line of backstitch and pass the needle under each stitch in turn, always in the same direction, without piercing the fabric.

FILLING STITCHES

If you decide not to follow my stitch placings exactly and instead choose to be free and creative with these designs, then it's important to choose the right stitch for the right size of space. For instance, satin stitch cannot be used for a large area as the stitches become too long and may get snagged and pull. Some of the stitches such as the buttonhole wheel are only suitable for larger spaces where they can be used as multiples, whereas the spiderweb stitch can be used as a single stitch to fill a small space or grouped to fill a large space.

*** TIP ***

When working "whipped" stitches, such as whipped backstitch, spiderweb, and woven rose, turn your needle around and insert through stitches with the eye end. This will stop you catching the fabric with the tip of the needle. Watch that sharp tip scratching the palm of your hand though!

1 Chain Stitch

This is a very versatile filling stitch for all sorts of shapes, with a wonderful texture that almost looks like knitting. Bring the needle up at A, then back down at the same point at B and out again at C, a stitch length along the line, with the tip of the needle over the loop of thread. Pull the thread through to form the first stitch, then take the needle back down through the loop at C and out again at D, a stitch length along the line, with the tip of the needle over the loop of thread once again. Work in close rows to fill the space; these can go up and down or spiraling from the outside in, depending on the size and shape of the area.

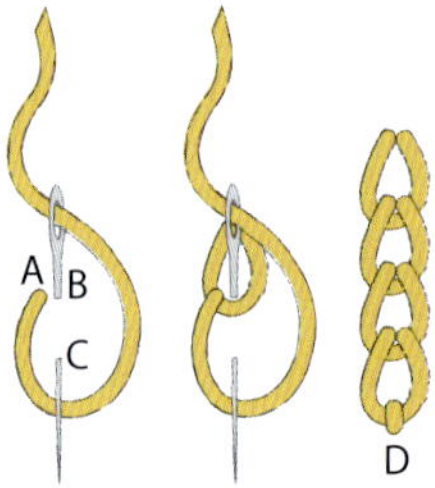

2 Satin Stitch

This classic stitch should lie flat and even and, if worked correctly, give the appearance of satin fabric. I usually find it easier to work from the middle of a shape outward. Bring the needle up through the fabric, just within the outline, and make a long stitch across the shortest side of the shape with the needle going down into the fabric on the other side of the shape just inside the outline. Bring the needle back out right next to the first stitch and make a parallel stitch that lies as close as possible to your first. Continue working out to the edge of the shape before returning to the center and working to the other edge. Satin stitches should be close together and parallel, with no gaps between them, to create a solid area of color. If you find a space between your stitches once you've finished, it's okay to go back and fill it with a single stitch.

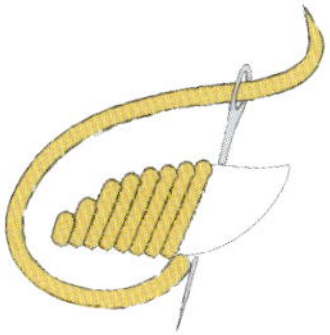

3 Colonial Knot

This is my favorite knot and the one I use throughout this book. Most embroidery patterns use French knots; but once you've mastered the colonial, it's hard to go back to a French. A colonial knot looks neater than a French and has a little swirl on the top; plus it also uses less thread. But it does take a little more practice before it feels natural. Bring your thread through to the front of the fabric at A. Hold the thread in your left hand and with your needle pointing away from you and to the left of the thread, slide the needle under the thread, toward the right. Wrap the thread over the needle tip to make a figure eight. Place the needle into the fabric at B, close to where it first emerged but not in the same hole. Before you pull it through, make sure the loop is snug around the shaft of the needle. Pull through to make the knot.

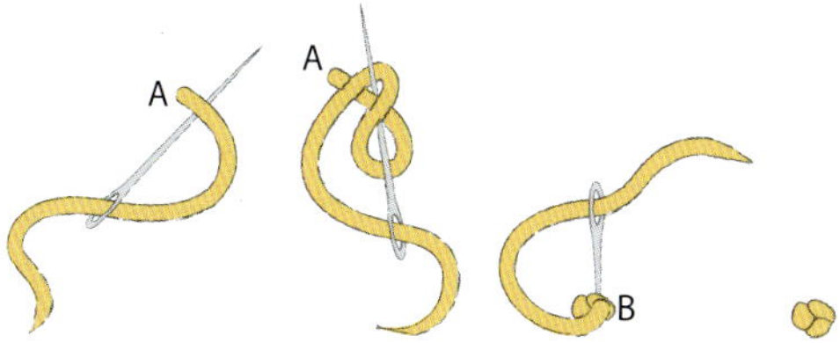

4 Seed Stitch and Double-Seed Stitch

Named because it gives the effect of a handful of seeds being scattered on the ground. The key is to make the stitches face in different directions. For variety I also like to work the double-seed stitch version. This little twist adds a small note of order to the randomness. Both these variations make a nice open (and quick!) filling stitch.

Bring the thread out at A and make a small straight stitch, inserting the needle at B. Then bring the needle out a short distance away and make another stitch of the same length at a different angle. Continue in this way to fill the area, trying to make your stitches as randomly placed as possible. To work a double seed, simply place pairs of stitches parallel to each other, but continue to place these double seeds in as many different directions as possible.

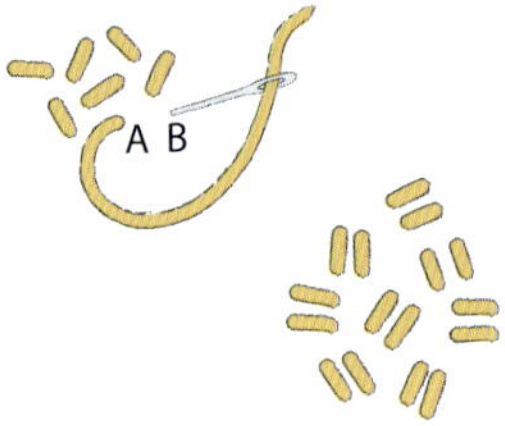

5 Running Stitch

This most basic of sewing stitches offers an interesting texture when worked in rows.

Working from right to left, bring the needle up to the right side of the work at A, then back down into the fabric a little way along the stitch line at B. Bring the needle out again about the same distance along at C. Repeat this action to form a line; use lines of running stitch to fill your shapes.

6 Split Stitch

This irregular filling stitch is like an overlapping backstitch. It gives a dense woven texture and can be used to fill larger areas than other solid stitches, such as satin stitch. For some reason I work my split stitch in the opposite direction to the orthodoxy, but it certainly works for me! Bring the needle up through the fabric at A, then back through at B, making a longer stitch then you would use for backstitch. Bring the needle up again at C, a half-stitch length away and bring down at D, in the center of the first stitch, splitting the fibers. Repeat with a few stitches in a row and then start to move in lines sideways, filling the space. This isn't such an exact stitch as the others; the idea is to get a nice even covering with no linen showing through.

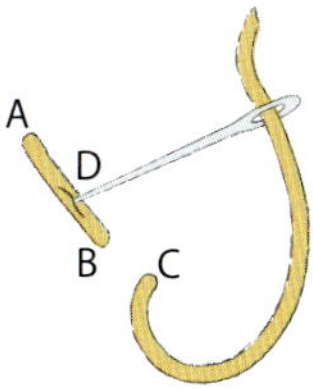

7 Bullion Knot

One of my favorite stitches, the bullion knot is very versatile and can be used as a filler or to add details to all sorts of embroidery designs. Bullion knots can have any number of thread wraps from two upward; the key is to match the number of wraps with the size of stitch (and the thickness of thread), which comes with practice. If your knot has a little hump and won't lie flat, then you need to make a longer stitch; and if you can see thread poking out at the ends of your knot, then your stitch is too long.

Bring your needle through at A and put it back through a stitch length away at B. The length of the stitch is dependent on the size of your bullion knot. Bring your needle out again at A, but do not pull your needle all the way through; instead, leave it halfway. Now start to wrap your thread around the tip of the needle. You may need to tilt the tip of the needle upward slightly to get these loops to stay on. Wrap the thread around the needle five or six times so that the coil of thread will cover the length of stitch. Place your thumb on the coiled thread and pull the needle through slowly and carefully so as not to disturb the coil. Insert the needle at B and gently pull the thread through until the bullion knot lies flat.

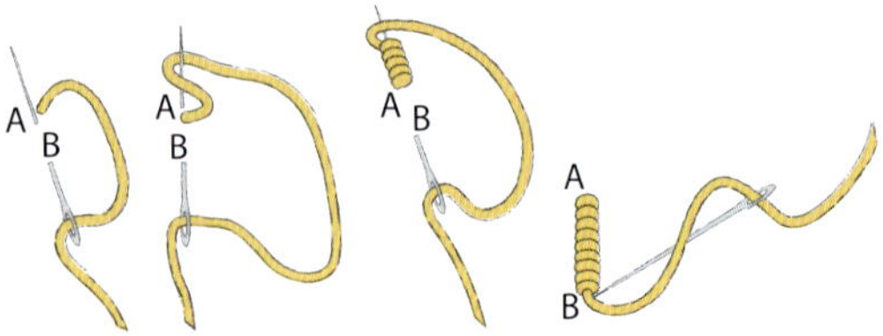

8 Laid Work

This name is rather a catch-all for a number of trellis-type crewelwork stitches that vary in degrees of intricacy. This is a simple couched version that adds a touch of Jacobean style while being able to retain a modern aesthetic. To give this stitch another modern twist, place your couching lines as vertical and horizontal rather than diagonal, which creates a square instead of the traditional diamond trellis.

Start by creating a grid over the chosen shape. Lay down all the threads that go in one direction first, placing your stitches just within the outline; then cross over the first layer with the second layer in the other direction. I always start with the center threads and work outward, lining up my stitches by eye. Using a contrasting thread, make tiny cross-stitches over the intersections of the laid threads, keeping your first and second stitches in the same order.

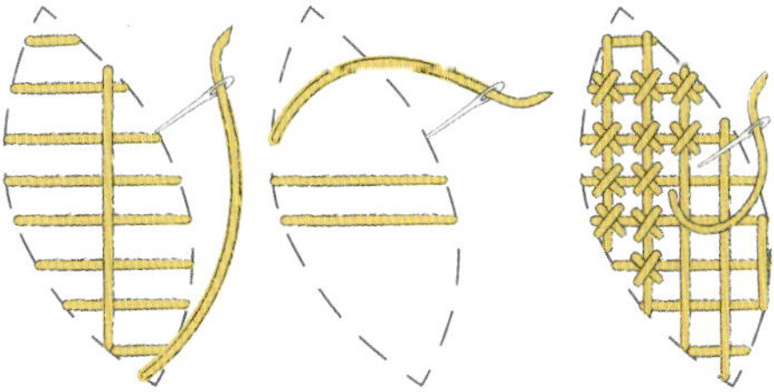

9 Cross-Stitch/Plus Stitch

Cross-stitch (or *plus stitch*) is one of the most basic stitches, but a very effective filler when used in rows. Bring the needle out at A and make a diagonal stitch to B. Bring the needle out at C, immediately below A and level with B. Make another diagonal stitch in line with A and B to complete the stitch. For the plus stitch version, simply turn your stitch to the side so that the straight stitches are vertical and horizontal rather than diagonal.

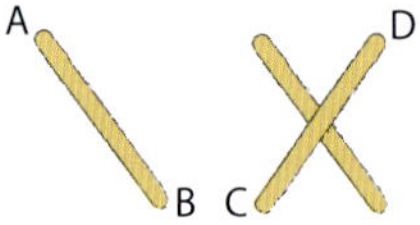

10 Star Stitch

Just one step up from cross-stitch. Start with a cross-stitch and add the star stitch on top by adding a vertical and a horizontal stitch.

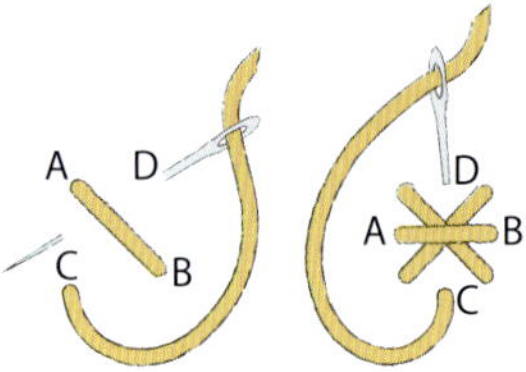

11 Felt Appliqué

The idea of using wool felt to fill some of the areas started with my first attempts at crewelwork. I simply thought that wool felt and wool threads belonged together. Mixing textures is a big part of this book, and using felt is a much quicker way to fill a space than embroidery, which is an added bonus. Save the felt appliqué option for your biggest areas and this will help you speed toward the finish line.

For the projects that use this technique, I have prepared patterns for you to use to cut your felt. If you want to use this technique with other designs, simply trace the shape from the pattern to create your own template.

Pin the felt in place and, using a matching thread, stitch to the fabric using small slip stitches that catch the edge of the felt. Don't place them too close to the edge, as this will shred your felt edges. Clover appliqué pins are helpful here as is Aurifil 80-weight thread, which is so fine it's almost invisible.

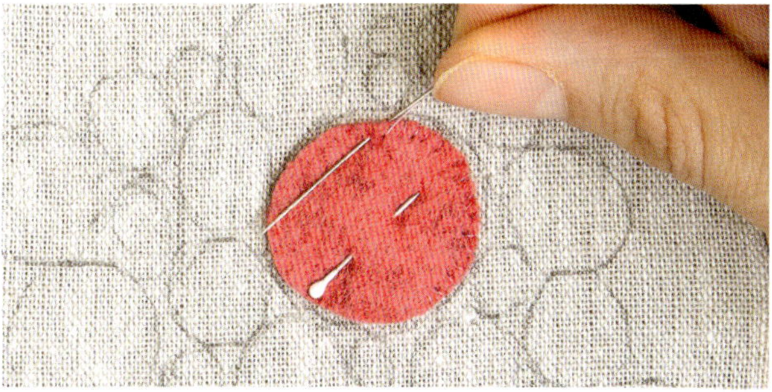

Felt appliqué

12 Closed Herringbone Stitch

Closed herringbone is a variety of herringbone where the stitch is worked so closely together that it forms a line of crossed stitches. By varying the length of the stitches, it can be worked to fill a shape.

Bring the thread through at A and insert the needle diagonally down to the right at B. Bring the thread through at C and insert the needle at D to make a cross. Bring the thread through at E immediately beside A and insert the needle at F, beside B. Bring the thread through at G, immediately beside C and insert the needle at H, beside D. Continue in this way to fill the shape, varying stitch lengths to fit.

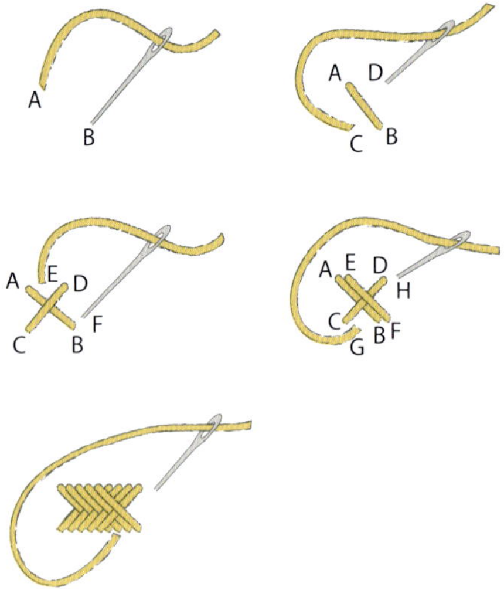

13 Spiderweb Stitch

Other names for this stitch include Spiderweb Backstitch, Whipped Wheel Stitch, and many more. It can be used to fill small spaces as in this design or grouped together to fill larger areas. It has a wonderful raised texture that works perfectly with the wool thread.

Bring the needle up at A and insert it at B, then bring the needle up at C and insert back in at B. Bring the needle up at D and then back in at B. Continue working alphabetically this way to make 8 spokes. Bring the needle up just next to the middle of the wheel, between 2 spokes, such as C and G as shown. Pass the needle over and under spoke C and then under spoke G. Next pass the needle over and under spoke G and then under spoke D. Continue in this way around the wheel, passing the needle over and under a spoke and then under the adjacent one until the wheel is full. If you are using this stitch to fill an irregular shape, you may find some of your spokes are longer than others and require a few more wraps of thread to fill them.

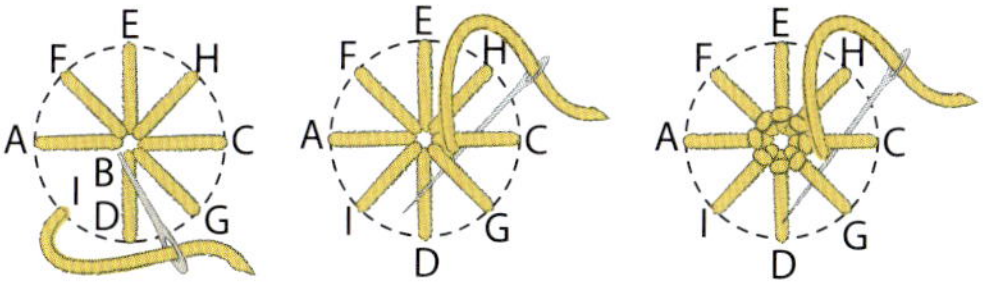

14 Vintage Rose

I encountered this stitch as a simple line drawing on a vintage stitch card and thought it was worth investigating. It creates a rose shape with quite realistic overlapping petals and is simple to stitch once you understand what is required. I teach this stitch often and advise my students to "Imagine the rose, and the rose will appear," and that seems to do the trick!

Begin by making 3 small straight stitches in a rough triangle shape with overlapping corners. Next make a ring of straight stitches around the triangle, crossing the corners and building up more sides. Bring the needle up alongside and at the middle of each stitch and lay the next stitch at a slight angle so that each stitch overlaps the one before and softens any edge points. Keep working outward in this way. The outline will become more rounded as it gets bigger, and a rose will emerge as if by magic! If you are filling an irregular shape, continue overlapping into the spaces at empty corners.

15 Lazy Daisy Stitch

Probably the cutest stitch there is and perennially popular, this is simply a group of detached chain stitches worked in a circle to create a flower shape. In some of the designs in this book, I've either left the center of the flower empty or, like here, added a single colonial knot in a contrast thread. I usually work my flowers with 6 petals, but 5 will do if you are running out of space (or thread!).

Bring the needle up at A and down at B, as close to A as possible. Bring the needle up at C and loop the thread around the needle, or make sure the needle is on top of the stitch loop as you bring it through. Insert the needle at D, passing the thread over the loop catching it down. Make another stitch beside this one but at a slight angle. Continue to place your petal stitches in a circle to complete the flower. Try not to pull your petals too tight or they will close up.

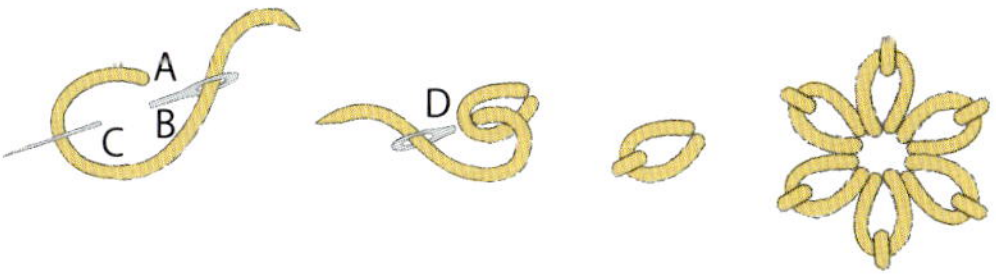

16 Fly Stitch

This simple V-shape stitch looks good worked in rows but can be adapted to fill shapes, as in the curved rows used in the Clamshell Pillow (page 51). Bring the needle up at A and down at B, but don't pull the thread tight; instead, leave a small loop. Bring the needle up at C where you want the point of the V to be and loop it over the stitch you made between A and B. Pull the thread and place your needle at D so that you catch down the V point to complete the stitch.

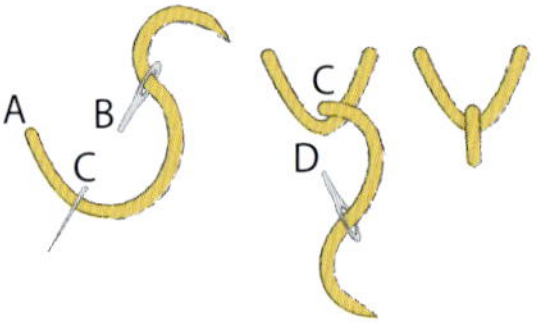

17 Woven Rose

Also known as a spiderweb rose, I call this a woven rose to distinguish it from the vintage rose. This is the more popular of the 2 roses and is very prevalent in modern designs. As with the spiderweb, this can be used to fill a small space in its entirety or individual roses can be grouped together.

Bring the needle up at A and insert it at B, then bring the needle up at C and insert back at B. Continue this way to create 5 spokes. Bring the needle up just next to the middle of the wheel and weave the thread over and under each spoke. Keep going in this way to completely cover the spokes. Finish by bringing the needle to the back.

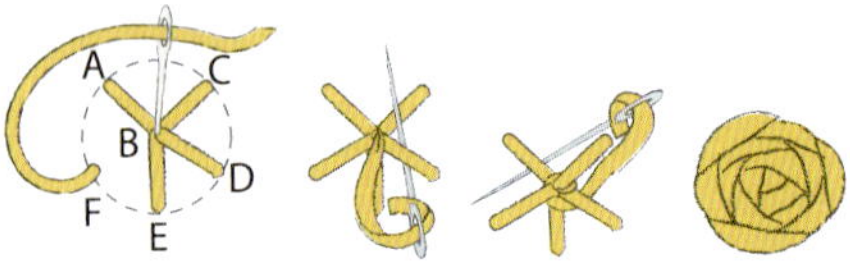

18 Blanket Stitch

Blanket stitch is a traditional stitch, used for binding and finishing the edges of a wool blanket. It can also be used as a way of joining pieces, as here, or as a decorative outline.

With the 2 pieces of felt together bring the needle out from between the pieces and through the felt on one side at A. Loop it over the felt edges and in again at B and back through to the first side at C, catching the loop of thread with the tip of the needle and pulling through to make the first stitch. Continue with the next stitch, bringing your thread over the felt edges and in at D and out again at E on the other side, catching the loop with your needle. Try to leave an even space between each stitch.

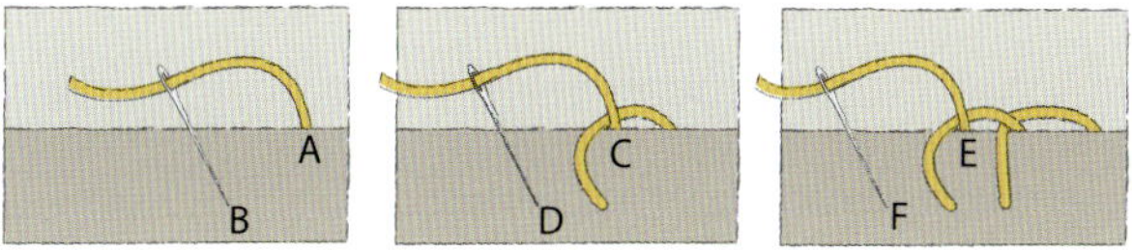

19 Buttonhole Wheel

When blanket stitch is used for a hand buttonhole, it is called buttonhole stitch, or as here, to make these sweet little wheels. This is another stitch that looks good grouped together as a filler. You always need to be firm and taut with this stitch as it is easy to "turn over" the edge stitches unless you keep an adequate stitch tension, though even if this happens, your wheels will still look cute.

Bring the needle up at A and down at B, but don't pull the thread tight; instead, leave a small loop. Bring the needle up at C, making sure it's inside the loop; you can use your finger to hold it in place. Insert the needle at B and bring it out at D to create the next spoke. Continue in this way to create the wheel. Finish with a tiny stitch joining at A.

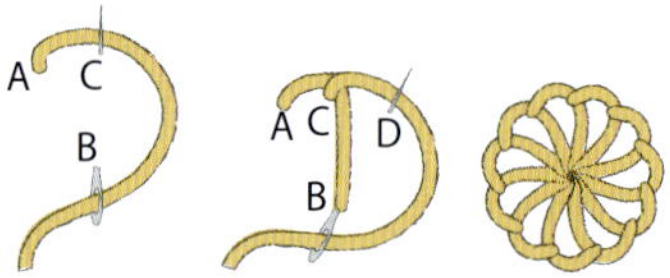

20 Straight Stitch

This is such a simple motion that it doesn't even require a diagram. It is simply one straight stitch, with the needle coming out at one point and going in again a stitch length away. In this project, we are using the straight stitches to add decorative rings and arches, and the width of the stitch is determined by the shape. Try to keep your stitches equal distance apart. I found it helpful to use the backstitches on the ring outline as a placement guide. Your stitches will need to slant slightly as they curve, especially around the tighter arches.

DOODLE HOOP

FINISHED PROJECT: 8″ × 8″ (20 × 20cm)
STITCHED AREA: 6″ × 6″ (15 × 15cm)

A simple doodle is the perfect way to start our crewel embroidery journey. If you relax and take your pencil for a walk, you can draw interesting patterns full of intersecting curves that give three-dimensional effects. Filling these different shapes with our basic stitches creates fabulous texture. I've used all my favorite filling stitches plus this project's bonus stitch: closed herringbone. Feel free to create your own doodle or use mine, but fill it with your chosen stitches and colors.

MATERIALS

Fabric: 11″ × 11″ (28 × 28cm) (I used Essex Linen Yarn-Dyed "Flax," a cotton/linen blend by Robert Kaufman Fabrics.)

Transfer pen/pencil

Wooden hoop: 8″ (20cm)

Thread: 1 each of Aurifil 12-weight wool 54-yard (50m) spools in the following colors:

A: black (8692)
B: peach (8212)
C: mint (8860)
D: yellow (8120)
E: raspberry red (8402)
F: cerise pink (8530)
G: magenta (8540)
H: white (8328)
I: blue (8810)
J: jade green (8870)

STITCHES

1 Chain (page 20): 2 strands

2 Satin (page 20): 2 strands

3 Colonial knot (page 21): 2 strands

4 Seed (page 22): 1 strand

5 Running (page 23): 1 strand

6 Split (page 23): 2 strands

12 Closed herringbone (page 28): 2 strands

CONSTRUCTION

Preparation

Using the Doodle Hoop design pattern (page 56) and following the tracing instructions (see Tracing, page 12), trace the image onto the fabric. Insert the fabric in the hoop (see Hooping, page 14).

Stitching

1. Using backstitch and 1 strand of A black (8962), stitch all the outlines.

2. Following the stitch guide, fill each section with different stitches as shown.

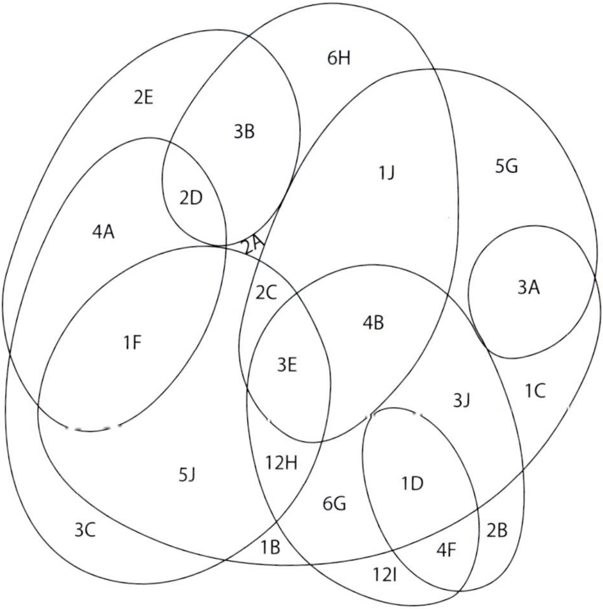

Stitch guide

Doodle hoop, close-up of texture

FINISHING

If necessary, remove the fabric from the hoop to erase any tracing lines and re-insert in the hoop. Follow the instructions to finish the hoop back (see Finishing a Hoop Back, page 15).

BUBBLES HOOP

FINISHED PROJECT: 7″ × 7″ (18 × 18cm)
STITCHED AREA: 5′½″ × 6″ (14 × 15cm)

The original spark for this whole book was a sampler embroidery that I made in 2019. Using wool thread and a wide variety of stitches created wonderful texture, especially when I added the felt appliqué details. I also enjoyed the mindful aspect of filling simple shapes with different stitches, and I have been planning to make another one ever since I finished the original. For this new version, I have concentrated on simple round bubble shapes and used a restricted palette of blues and greens to give an aquatic feel. The cotton fabric is a hand-dyed cotton, which gives extra movement to the piece.

MATERIALS

Fabric: 10″ × 10″ (25 × 25cm) (I used Hand-Dyed Osnaburg in "Light Ocean," a cotton fabric with a linen-like texture by Fiber on a Whim.)

Transfer pen/pencil

Wooden hoop: 7″ (17.5cm)

Wool felt scraps: Green / blue / turquoise shades

Thread: 1 each of Aurifil 12-weight wool 54-yard (50m) spools in the following colors:

Outline: charcoal (8083)
A: dark green (8880)
B: sky blue (8810)
C: mint (8860)
D: jade green (8875)
E: leaf green (8962)
F: grass green (8965)
G: teal (8870)
H: variegated green (8007)
I: pale turquoise (8823)
J: dark blue (8740)
K: pale green (8860)
L: pale yellow (8130)
M: variegated blue (8009)
N: variegated turquoise (8008)
O: turquoise (8803)

STITCHES

1 Chain (page 20): 2 strands

2 Satin (page 20): 2 strands

3 Colonial knot (page 21): 2 strands

4 Seed (page 22): 1 strand

8 Laid work (page 25): 2 strands

10 Star (page 26): 1 strand

11 Felt appliqué (page 27)

13 Spiderweb (page 29): 2 strands

14 Vintage rose (page 30): 2 strands

CONSTRUCTION

Preparation

Using the Bubbles Hoop design pattern (page 57) and following the tracing instructions (see Tracing, page 12), trace the image onto the fabric. Insert the fabric in the hoop (see Hooping, page 14).

Stitching

1. Using backstitch and 1 strand of charcoal (8083), stitch all the outlines except those around the felt appliqué (#11) circles.

2. Following the stitch guide, fill each section with different stitches as shown.

3. Using the Bubbles Hoop bubbles/circles appliqué patterns (page 58), cut out 6 different felt bubbles/circles. Pin in place over the matching circles and stitch down with matching thread (see Felt Appliqué, page 27). Using 1 strand of charcoal (8083), stitch the outlines around the felt.

Bubbles hoop, close-up of texture

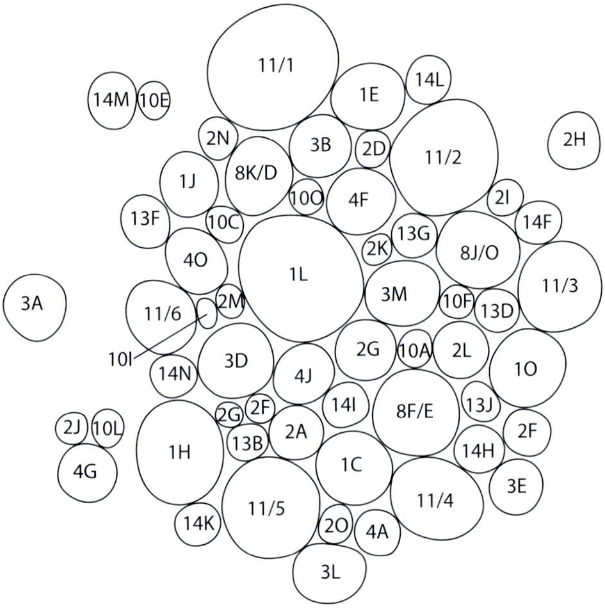

Stitch guide

FINISHING

If necessary, remove the fabric from the hoop to erase any tracing lines and re-insert in the hoop. Follow the instructions to finish the hoop back (see Finishing a Hoop Back, page 15).

Honeycomb Hoop

FINISHED PROJECT: 10″ × 10″ (25 × 25cm)
STITCHED AREA: 7″ × 9″ (18 × 23cm)

For my geometric patterns, the starting point often stems from one of the many patchwork patterns that are dear to my heart. We are going back to basics with the very first patchwork I ever did, age ten years old. Nowadays we call this ***English paper piecing****, but back in the 1970s it was the only patchwork I knew. Hexagons are such a pleasing shape and filled with all those woolly textures, they started to remind me of honeycomb, so I just had to add a bee! This also led to the honey-toned color palette which, along with the brown background, makes the whole thing warm and comforting.*

MATERIALS

Fabric: 13″ × 13″ (33 × 33cm) (I used Essex Linen Yard-Dyed "Leather," a cotton/linen blend by Robert Kaufman Fabrics.)

Transfer pen/pencil

Wooden hoop: 10″ (25cm)

Thread: 1 each of Aurifil 12-weight wool 54-yard (50m) spools in the following colors:

Outline hexagons:
dark brown (8088)
Outline bee wings:
pale gray (8605)
A: variegated yellow (8001)
B: pale yellow (8130)
C: yellow (8120)
D: dark yellow (8135)
E: pale orange (8205)
F: peach (8212)
G: orange (8235)
H: dark orange (8220)
I: variegated orange (8003)
J: black (8692)
K: gray (8082)

STITCHES

1 Chain (page 20): 2 strands

2 Satin (page 20): 2 strands

3 Colonial knot (page 21): 2 strands

4 Double-seed (page 22): 1 strand

5 Running (page 23): 1 strand

6 Split (page 23): 2 strands

8 Laid work (page 25): 2 strands

15 Lazy daisy (page 31): 1 strand

17 Woven rose (page 32): 2 strands

19 Buttonhole wheel (page 34): 1 strand

CONSTRUCTION

Preparation

Using the Honeycomb Hoop pattern (page 59) and following the tracing instructions (see Tracing, page 12), trace the image onto the fabric. Insert the fabric in the hoop (see Hooping, page 14).

Stitching

1. Using backstitch and 1 strand of dark brown (8361), stitch all the hexagon outlines.

2. Following the stitch guide, fill each hexagon with different stitches as shown.

3. To add variety, work your chain stitch and laid work in different directions each time they are used.

4. Work the body of the bee in satin stitch, using 2 strands of thread and alternating black and yellow stripes. The antennae are stitched using a single strand of black thread and backstitch. The legs are outlined with a double strand of black thread and backstitch. The eyes are double-stranded colonial knots in black.

5. For the wings, outline with a single strand of pale gray thread (8600) and a backstitch, filling with rows of running stitch in a single strand of gray thread.

Honeycomb hoop, close-up of texture

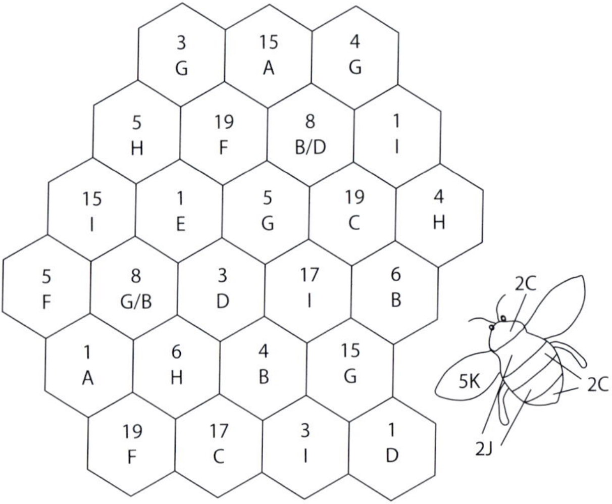

Stitch guide

Finishing

If necessary, remove the fabric from the hoop to erase any tracing lines and re-insert in the hoop. Follow the instructions to finish the hoop back (see Finishing a Hoop Back, page 15).

MANDALA HOOP

FINISHED PROJECT: 10" × 10" (25.5 × 25.5cm)
STITCHED AREA: 8½" × 8½" (21.5 × 21.5cm)

I find embroidery very meditative and mindful, and so this was an obvious choice for a design subject. A mandala is a geometric design that represents wholeness and the universe. Through contemplation to the point of saturation, a mandala is thought to help you gain a meditative state of mind. If this is correct, then with all the hours you will spend stitching this design, you should be very calm and relaxed by the end of it!

This design stands out from the others as it uses heavy, dense stitches rather than decorative ones, and the choice of both stitches and colors is more restricted. To stop the stitched areas appearing too saturated, I used the outlining charcoal thread to create decorative bands that break up the blocks of color. This also means I can introduce you to the most straightforward stitch in the book as this project's bonus stitch. I have chosen bright, jewel-like thread colors and another of the hand-dyed Osnaburg cottons in a warm sunset shade. These elements go together to evoke a new age hippie vibe full of peace and love. Hang this on your wall and gaze at it when you need to de-stress.

MATERIALS

Fabric: 13″ × 13″ (33 × 33cm) (I used Hand-Dyed Osnaburg in "Day Lily," a cotton fabric with a linen-like texture by Fiber on a Whim.)

Transfer pen/pencil

Bright pink felt: 10″ × 10″ (25.5 × 25.5cm)

Wooden hoop: 10″(25cm)

Thread: 1 each of Aurifil 12-weight wool 54-yard (50m) spools in the following colors:

Outline: charcoal (8083)
A: pale turquoise (8823)
B: turquoise (8810)
C: orange (8235)
D: magenta (8540)
E: hot pink (8530)

STITCHES

1 Chain (page 20): 2 strands

2 Satin (page 20): 2 strands

3 Colonial knot (page 21): 2 strands

6 Split (page 23): 2 strands

11 Felt appliqué (page 27)

13 Spiderweb (page 29): 2 strands

20 Straight (page 34): 1 strand

CONSTRUCTION

Preparation

Using the Mandala Hoop design pattern (page 60) and following the tracing instructions (see Tracing, page 12), trace the image onto the fabric. Insert the fabric in the hoop (see Hooping, page 14).

Stitching

1. Using backstitch and 1 strand of charcoal (8083), stitch all the outlines except those around the felt appliqué (#11) outer dome shapes. Use 1 strand of the same thread to stitch straight stitches to create decorative rings and arches as indicated in the guide. Use 2 strands of the same thread to fill the adjacent ring with equally spaced colonial knots, along with alternate borders on the outer arches.

2. Following the stitch guide, fill each section with different stitches as shown.

3. Using the Mandala Hoop appliqué pattern (page 60), cut out 8 felt pieces. Pin them in place over each #11 shape as indicated in the stitch guide and stitch down with matching thread (see Felt Appliqué, page 27). Using 1 strand of charcoal (8083), stitch the outlines around the felt.

Mandala hoop, close-up of texture

Stitch guide

Finishing

If necessary, remove the fabric from the hoop to erase any tracing lines and re-insert it in the hoop. Follow the instructions to finish the hoop back (see Finishing a Hoop Back, page 15).

CLAMSHELL PILLOW

FINISHED PROJECT: 12″ × 12″ (30.5 × 30.5cm)
STITCHED AREA: 10″ × 10″ (25.5 × 25.5cm)

Our last design is a big one, and it includes almost all the stitches we've been practicing so far. It was inspired by yet another favorite patchwork pattern and one that works particularly well as a pillow. I decided to create an ombré effect by stitching each row in a different shade, which washes down through the colors in a gentle ripple. I love this colorwash effect and have made similar ombré clamshell pillows using fabric. Using the same stitch and color for each clamshell in a row creates a new twist on the sampler genre and one that works well for interior decor. This would make a special small pillow to adorn a bed or a statement chair, one suited more to decoration rather than heavy usage.

MATERIALS

Fabric: 15″ × 35″ (38 × 90cm) (I used Essex Linen Yarn-Dyed "Bleached White," a cotton/linen blend by Robert Kaufman Fabrics.)

Transfer pen/pencil

Wooden hoop: 10″ (25cm)

Pillow form: 12″ (30.5cm)

Thread: 1 each of Aurifil 12-weight wool 54-yard (50m) spools in the following colors:

Outline: brown (8088)
A: mauve (8553)
B: pale pink (8574)
C: dusky pink (8431)
D: orange (8215)
E: peach (8212)
F: yellow (8130)
G: lemon (8120)
H: mint (8860)
I: pale turquoise (8865)
J: turquoise (8803)
K: petrol blue (8735)

STITCHES

1 Chain (page 20): 2 strands

3 Colonial knot (page 21): 2 strands

4 Double-seed (page 22): 1 strand

5 Running (page 23): 1 strand

8 Laid work (page 25): 2 strands

10 Star (page 26): 1 strand

13 Spiderweb (page 29): 2 strands

15 Lazy daisy (page 31): 1 strand

16 Fly (page 32): 1 strand

17 Woven rose (page 32): 2 strands

19 Buttonhole wheel (page 34): 1 strand

CONSTRUCTION

Preparation

From the Essex linen fabric, cut a square 15″ × 15″ (38 × 38cm). Using the Clamshell Pillow design pattern (page 61) and following the tracing instructions (see Tracing, page 12), trace the image onto the fabric. Insert the fabric in the hoop (see Hooping, page 14).

Stitching

1. Using backstitch and 1 strand of brown (8320), stitch all the outlines.

2. Following the stitch guide, fill each row of clamshells with different stitches as shown. Each clamshell in a row is filled by

the same stitch and shade as indicated in the first clamshell on the guide.

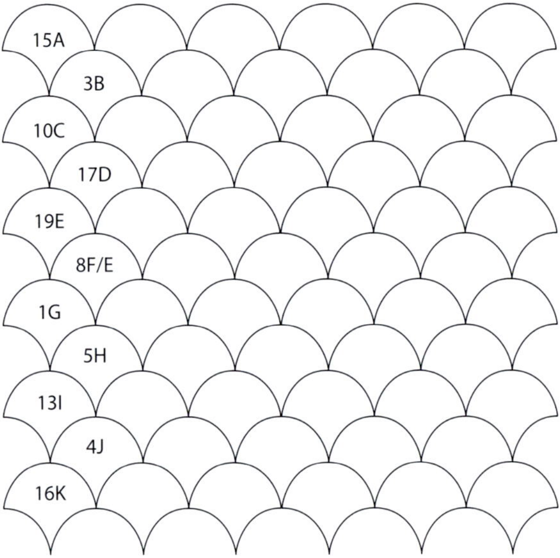

Stitch guide

Make the Pillow

1. Remove from the hoop to erase any tracing lines and press carefully. Trim to a 13″ × 13″ (33 × 33cm) square.

2. From the remainder of the linen fabric, cut 2 rectangles 10″ × 13″ (25.5 × 33cm). Turn over a ½″ (1cm) hem twice on a

Clamshells embroidery, close-up of texture

13″ (33cm) side on one of the pieces. Pin and then stitch along to hem. Repeat with the other backing piece. Press.

3. Lay the embroidered front, right side up. Lay the 2 back pieces on top, right sides down, overlapping the seamed edges in the center. Pin all the way around and stitch, using a ½″ (1cm) seam allowance. Snip the corners, turn right side out, and press. Insert a pillow form.

PATTERNS

Doodle Hoop (page 35)—design motif

Enlarge 200%

Full-size downloadable pattern:
tinyurl.com/20558-patterns-download

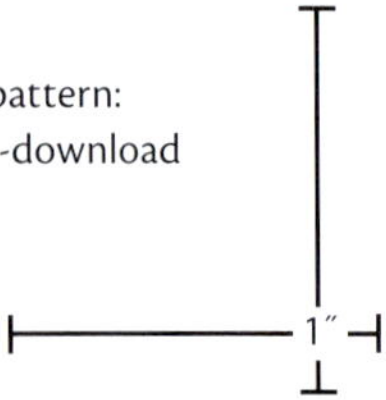

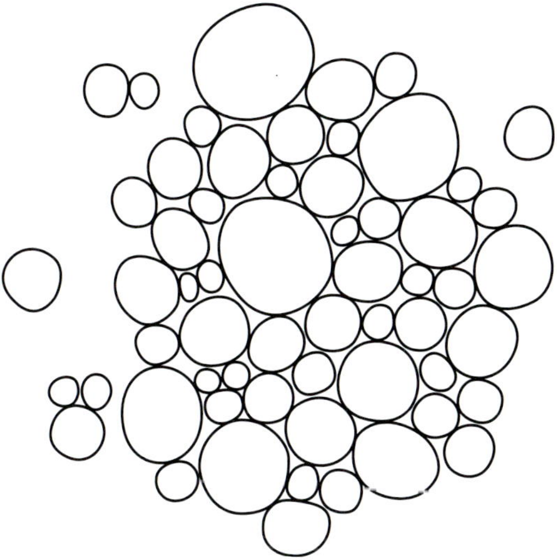

Bubbles Hoop (page 39)—design motif

Enlarge 200%

Full-size downloadable pattern:
tinyurl.com/20558-patterns-download

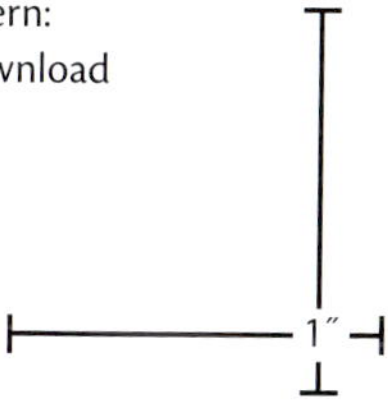

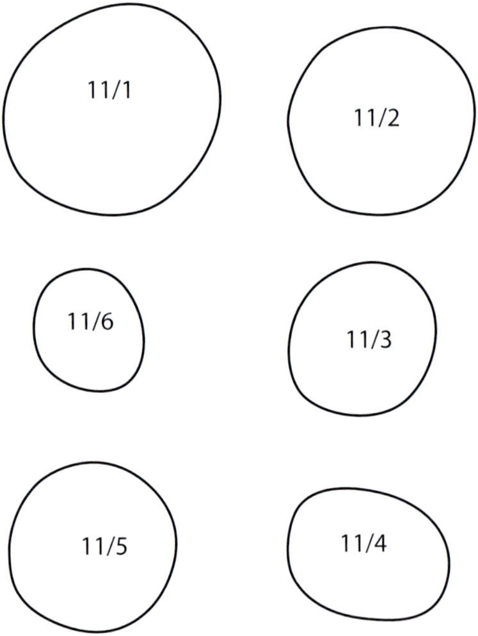

Bubbles Hoop (page 39)—bubbles/circle appliqués

1″

Honeycomb Hoop (page 43)—design motif

Enlarge 200%

Full-size downloadable pattern:
tinyurl.com/20558-patterns-download

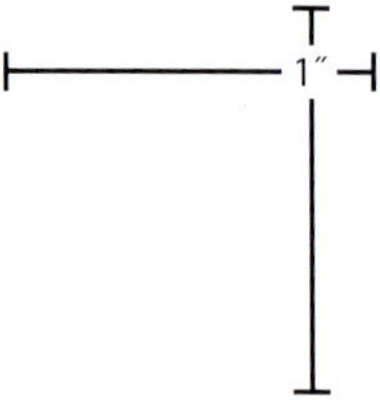

Mandala Hoop (page 47)—mandala appliqué

Mandala Hoop (page 47)—design motif

Enlarge 200%

Full-size downloadable pattern: tinyurl.com/20558-patterns-download

Clamshell Pillow—design motif (page 51)

Enlarge 200%

Full-size downloadable pattern:
tinyurl.com/20558-patterns-download

Publisher: Amy Barrett-Daffin

Creative Director: Gailen Runge

Senior Editor: Roxane Cerda

Editors: Kathryn Patterson and Gailen Runge

Technical Editor: Del Walker

Cover/Book Designer: April Mostek

Production Coordinator: Zinnia Heinzmann

Illustrator: Valyrie Gillum

Photography Coordinator: Rachel Ackley

Photography by Estefany Gonzalez and Lauren Herberg of C&T Publishing, Inc., unless otherwise noted

Published by C&T Publishing, Inc., P.O. Box 1456, Lafayette, CA 94549

Printed in the USA

10 9 8 7 6 5 4 3 2 1

ABOUT THE AUTHOR

Jo Avery lives in the countryside near Edinburgh in Scotland surrounded by woodland and wildlife. She began her career in textiles and entrepreneurship at age 21 with her first business, Cleopatra's Needle, which designed and produced needlepoint kits. She learned to make quilts soon after and continued to pursue this as a hobby while bringing up a family and partnering her husband, Jonathan Avery in their furniture and retail business.

A decade ago, she discovered quilting blogs and began her own. A whole new career sprang from this: teaching crafts and designing quilt and embroidery patterns.

She now teaches far and wide, designs quilts and embroideries for a number of magazines, and organizes quilt retreats, both physical and virtual. She is one-third of The Thread House collective and is a certified Aurifilosopher. Her books, *New Patchwork & Quilting Basics* and *Modern Crewel Embroidery*, were published by Stash Books.

Visit Jo online and follow on social media!
Website: stitchgathering.co.uk
Blog: joavery.co.uk
Instagram: @joaverystitch